A message from Sonia B.

This is my reflection on the happenings over our restricted movement. For me it was a time of rest, recuperation and learning self-love, which might resonate with others. At the same time, there are many who may have found it to be a troublesome and mentally draining period for them. I do hope that my little offering has some kind of reflective meaning for you all.

My love and God blessings.
Sonia B.

The world is on lockdown sleep   3

Change.   5

Hey man!!   7

Clap Clap Clap your hands   9

Living a Lie   10

You called   12

Happiness   13

Freewheeling   14

Set all animals free.   15

The bane of my life.   17

Love   18

My dear father.   19

My Two MOTHERS.   21

Loving me   23

Black lives matter!   25

Black on Black   26

Did we say you can stay?   28

Are we a welcome visitor or an invader?   30

Jesus Jesus   32

The Morning Lullaby.   33

The Wooden Box   34

What say us?   35

Tek weh no fi yuh   36

My Twilight Years   37

You are running the Hackney Half Marathon No way!!!!   38

Trust You?   42

We got no wifi   43

Crying silently.   45

He is a flirt.   46

Myself   47

Jamaica   48

About the author   50

The world is on lockdown sleep

The world is on lockdown sleep
The world is on lockdown sleep while God do his
work

FATHER GOD I HEAR YOUR CALL

The signs are plain to see there can be no dote

FATHER GOD I HEAR YOUR CALL

The word, the light, the presence on earth

FATHER GOD I HEAR YOUR CALL

Heaven will rejoice so too will the universe

FATHER GOD I HEAR YOUR CALL

For our God is truly walking on this earth

FATHER GOD I HEAR YOUR CALL

Signs and wonders everyone can see

FATHER GOD I HEAR YOUR CALL,

Are you ready to see the God Almighty,

FATHER GOD I HEAR YOUR CALL

Don't delay the time is now
Bow down to the Lord and make your vows

FATHER GOD I HEAR YOUR CALL

Be ready to live as one, for on Calvary his blood
was shed.

FATHER GOD I HEAR YOUR CALL

Death is no more, for us he won, life eternal and not
just for some

FATHER GOD I HERE YOUR CALL

I heed your word, in your bosom I want to be, from
now and All eternity

FATHER GOD I AM GLAD YOU CALLED.

Change.

We all now have change thrown our way
We are now crying our old way of life has gone
away
We are all feeling the pain of change, is it here to
stay.

We are challenging the need to remain the same.

Tell me one and all, is this because we don't want
to suffer brain strain?
Change
Change

We feel the powder of the chain pulling at our heart.
It drains the pain of change.
I gladly refrain from being disdain and hope the
change I will embrace.
My brain my heart will quietly sustain
Accepting the need for change.

Brave are we
We clap for love
We clap for thanks In the mid we clap and march
for change
We hope justice will prevail.
But do we all understand why we make this stand?
Change
Change

Is this the new plan?
Rainbow drawing signpost of change.
Tomorrow we'll wake up to forget,
Or will we?
Will we?
Will we?
Change.
Change.

Hey man!!

Crossing the road all dress up Corona style.
A man on his bicycle want to quicken my stride,
Shouted "Hey man, get out of the road!" Sounded
his bell and shouted.

I didn't look, I told myself what the hell.
The Corona uniform dressing have stolen my
identity,
Am I now a man I begin to fret.
I looked at myself in the mirror once home.
This is slander not just on me, but on corona dress
code.
Corona, Corona you can't steal it all,
My clothes do not say who I am, this is not the plan.
We will dress to protect, man, woman, girl or boy or
LGBTQ+
I will not digress.

Our sex we'll boast when we boot you, bad, bad,
corona from our shore.
Corona, Corona we shall show you the door for
sure.
Our sex will be in doubt no more. Man, woman, boy
or girl
Care for mistake no more we will find a cure.
Corona, Corona you will be no more.
The man on his bicycle should have no doubt
Woman I am so he can shout, "Hey woman get out

of the road",
Corona then you will see. we will surely banish you
to the sea.
No more will you be,
Universally we will all be free.

Clap Clap Clap your hands

Clap Clap Clap your hands for joy, because you know that our saviour lives. (repeat chorus)

Many a soul will be saved meeting our God face to face. Chorus.

Give thanks for that special day
Make ready people get up and sing God praises. Chorus.

God lives, yes he lives. Jesus lives, yes he lives. The holy spirit lives, Yes he lives. Chorus

Oh yes he lives, oh yes he lives.
We can be glad one and all and ,clap our hand with joy

Because our saviour rains. Chorus.

Living a Lie

A veil of deceit
Promiscuous teenager-adult
Being mentally and physically abuse as a child and
as an adult
Disobedient
No ambition
Lied
Cheat

LIVING A LIE

When did I turn the corner?
I said turn the corner because I am now on that
road to recovery.
I wrote about finding peace, is it out there?

LIVING A LIE

A life that sees me lose control of my very being,
lost track of reality.
The past becomes my haunting present with no
clear road of a future.

LIVING A LIE

Is one in denials? or clueless?
Trauma, Trauma, Trauma!!
How do I find release?
How do I ease the pain?
How do I replace what has been taken away?
The question goes on and on.

LIVING A LIE

I find that I can't change the past but with my belief
in the Almighty God I can live with it by living in the
present.
The past belongs to God
The present is now
The future also belongs to the father.

"LIVE YOUR BEST LIFE ON PURPOSE" - *Gbaby*.

Today as I wrote this piece I feel a sense of pride in
knowing that I have really got to this stage in my life
when I can truly say thanks to God and fully feel it
and own it.

You called

You called me several times
You called me several times before I take your
hands
You called me several times I fail to understand
You called me several times how patient you have
been
You called me several times oh Lord I could not see
You called me several times my Lord oh how you
care for me
You called me several times my Lord your thirst for
me is true
You called me several times to you dear Lord I will
give my all
You called me several times on the cross you lay
down your life
You called me several times to be with the risen
Christ
You called me several times believe for life eternal
you won for me
You called me several times my Lord I am your now
and ever more
You called me several times dear Lord the victory
you have won
You called me several times oh precious light of
everlasting grace
You called me several times.
I bow to your redeeming love.

Happiness

Happiness is waking up in the morning.
Happiness is smiling at people who cross your path
And they smile back.
Happiness is saying thank you.
Happiness is feeling the warmth of the cup of hot drink
Between your palms.
Happiness is love first kiss.
Happiness is feeling the beating heart next to yours.
Happiness is a long embrace from your loved ones.
Happiness is a relaxing bath.
Happiness is listening to music while doing house work
And dancing.

Happiness is saying I love you.
Happiness is reaching out to others with a helping hand.
Happiness is a warm hug.
Happiness is laughing out loud.
Happiness is embracing life.
Happiness is being happy with being alive.
Happiness is saying hello.
Happiness is loving yourself.
Happiness is hearing the birds sing.
Happiness is being fulfilled, loving who you are.
Happiness is being you

Freewheeling

Freewheeling

A kiss and an embrace
Freewheeling

My chain slips when I slam the brakes
Freewheeling

You stand still Oh my dear! it feel like I am on stilts
Freewheeling

I am once more free
The breeze
The trees
Freewheeling

My love, your bosom will catch me.
Freewheeling

The lap of luxury Freewheeling.

Set all animals free.

This Coronavirus have us going potty
We mourn we wallow in self-pity
Let just think of our dear friends we call the dumb
animals
We cage them, we fence them up, we put them in
glass tank,
We put them in a 12-foot pond.

Just stop and think folks, a 160kg gorilla in a space
as big as your
Front room gash year in year out,
Without any doubt they must feel mentally space
out.

Think of a Lion, a Tiger, a Whale or even a Shark.
Not to mention Dolphins, Rhino or hippo.
Do I need to go on naming them all?
The message I am sure is clear for all to see
The goldfish in a bowl and the elephant are not
able to go to the Water hole.

Can you now see the story needed to be told?
What say our friends need the open sea the mud
hole on
The sunny terrain, the chance to fly above the
plane.
Humans like to say free as a bird let our feathered
friend stop feeling the strains.

Give them their freedom to make the sky their domain.

Come on guys, the power in our hand, let free all animals in the land.
Stop giving them the hell we can't seem to stand, just for
These few months in isolation.
Corona sure show us restriction of freedom should be banded for all the dumb animal in the land.
We the wise animal should make it our plan to free all our dumb species in our land.

The bane of my life.

The bane of my life.
Do you say pips?
Tiny microscopic pips
Ever eat a blueberry with false teeth in?
Talking about spitting and washing
The bane or should I say pain of my life.
Can't stop spitting them out.
Got to shout get out mi mouth.

Love

Love like the raindrops
Shower down then disappear.

My love but like a stream
Never more to cease
Tis my sweet dear not
Your welly a hole in the pair.

Hop on air fill puddle fare
The raindrops colour water Glisten on the rocky
shore
The love on your muddy welly stood up
Beneath the alcove of despair.
The raindrop of distant hemisphere.

My dear father.

My dear father how I have long for just a glance.
How I have long to see the colour of your eyes.
How I have long for your arms to hold me tight.
How I have long for you to greet me with a smile.
How I have long to hear you say my daughter I love you.
How I have long to hug and kiss you.
How I have long to sit around your table.
My dear father.
How I would have love to bounce on your knee.
How I long to be in your house.
How I have long to learn your ways.
How I have long to be part of your days.
My dear father now that your eyes are closed, I am loss your favourite food I do not know,
Your favourite colour I am not sure,
Your wisdom I no longer able to share.
My dear father I never did hold your hand.
Have never been included in your plans.
Did not know your real name till after you were gone.
My dear father.
I look forward to hear your favourite story,
When we meet on that day of glory.
My dear father our story may have never been told,
But now father rest assured though you are in slumber sleep.
My love for you is wide awake and with me you will

Always be a father that I adore for evermore.
REST IN PEACE DADDY.

My Two MOTHERS.

My birth mother and my nurturing mother.
From my biological mother I learnt to cook
macaroni and cheese,
Fry chicken and mash potatoes.
From my nurturing mum I learnt life skills.
Thank you, pardon me and please.
Mum tall giant of a woman to my short stature
growing up,
As a child.
She stands majestically in her plaid skirt, colourful
blouse, her dark black
Hair plait in four plaits, two at the back of her head
and two at the front
On her face nestles either side of her cheeks.
Always called me by my given full birth names
when I am in trouble.
At other times she just gave me the look!
You automatically knew no mess or else.
You then knew no nonsense or you could be
ancient.
Keeping a beautiful home was a must.
Smelling sweet,
Nice and shiny red polish floor lovely white iron bed
spreads,
Flowers adorning the house.
Scrumptious smelling food wafting the
neighbourhood pot full
With enough to feed the whole country.

You must not be short whoever calls.
Remembering to empty all pockets before you
wash the clothes,
Treats the collars and cuffs spread white to bleach
in the sun,
When hung on line should dazzle the onlooker.
Always save for that rainy day.
Always have that suitcase packed with essentials
ready for the hospital.
Always show a loving heart.
Live good, watch and pray.
Save the best clothes, hats shoes for church
And attend all funerals in the district whether you
know them or not.
Respect others, especially your elders.
Aunt Dine was a one in a million, marvelous mum.
Love my two mothers.

Loving me

Dance girl dance
Dance girl dance

Feet aching, pulse racing

Dance girl dance
Dance girl dance

Shimmer and shaking, heart pumping

Dance girl dance
Dance girl dance

Music playing, bass guitar strumming

Dance girl dance
Dance girl dance

Loving me

Dance girl dance
Dance girl dance

What do you see

Dance girl dance
Dance girl dance

Laugh, cry, take a drink and smile

Dance girl dance
Dance girl dance

Love your style, love your pride,

Dance girl dance
Dance girl dance

Loving me, take baby step do not digress

Dance girl dance
Dance girl dance

In a trance embracing, fully knowing.

Dance girl dance
Dance girl dance

The love within the love without

Dance girl dance
Dance girl dance

Knowing its overflowing
Loving me, discover me, knowing me

Dance girl dance
Dance girl dance
Love me.

Black lives matter!

From as long as things been record
Having Black skin has sting.
No reading, no writing, washing, cleaning the yard.
Look at your white counterpart, man for our life they
got no regard.
Take us from our homelands, put us in chains
Try to take our skins off with cat-o-nine cane.
Lord when will we stop feeling the pain.
Many try, many die, freedom what freedom not
even master of our yard.
Police brutality, government ignorance, world
acceptance!
Do we carry on turning a blind eye come on
brothers and sisters
Together we stand.

BLACK LIVES MATTER.

We are as good as our white brothers and sisters
even those who don't give a damn. Stop kneeling
on our necks, stop hurting our kind, what will it take
for us to find,
Peace
Peace between races,
peace with many faces,
it's time to unite as one,
It's time all this is done!

Black on Black

Black on Black why do we attack our brothers
Gun, knife in the belly, in the back just think of that

Black on **Black**

When will we learn, do we now feel it's our turn To
give.
The hurt the pain, do we forget our fore parent
disgrace,
The woe and years of suffering they endure in hope
of freeing our race.
Oh dear God are we insane!!

Black on **Black**

We should stand proud we should be strong by
remembering
Their fight we can't go wrong.

Black on **Black**

Let take stock we are our brother keeper and that's
a fact
We should be each other's rock.

Black on **Black**

Brother we would hope from now on you got my

back.

Black on **Black**

Black on Black my brother we are from the same stock.

Did we say you can stay?

Mi come a England to learn proper English,
To learn fi build flat and sleep ina beautiful, stylish
house.
But mi dear when de boat land
Mi plan sink ina the sand.
No where to rest mi weary bone
NO BLACK
NO DAWG
NO IRISH
Greet mi a every door.
Mi slum it and wok for years, mi bill big houses but
mi can't go through di doors.
Time pass by mi get a lickle boat hole to call mi
own.
Laying ina mi bed mi here a tump a di front door.
Jump outta bed to see who a bruk down mi door.
The chap said to mi "come with me mate,
Your paper I would like to see".
We believe you have no right to stay in this country.
The plane and 2000 pounds coming your way.
Before mi have time fi open mi mouth,
The cell door slam shut, Ah wha happen there.
Not even a phone call mi afi wait fi daybreak.
In jail mi find mi self without bail.
Man mi a fi prove mi right fi stay ina di land mi call
home fi years.

The land mi gave mi sweat and blood.

The land mi bring up mi daughter and mi son.
The land mi call home fi sixty years.
The land mi come to know and love.
Rest assure mi no done,
Mi nah go sit here and twiddle mi tumbs
This a case mi a go won.

Are we a welcome visitor or an invader?

In 1948 the invitation was sent out
Come to the motherland and find work
Come alone, come with your family,
Come one, come all
We at the motherland is at a lost the country has
taken a downward fall after the war.
On June 22nd the first boat dock at Tilbury dock
They were there with camera and microphone in
hand
We were all excided reaching England
This beautiful land that is paved with gold.
Proverbial gold
Sadly to say we should have board the boat back
that same day
Welcome we were not!
Nowhere to rest our weary head
Our children segregated send away to so call
special school
Branded a backward fool
We did the job we came to do we were frown upon
Sworn at and called names and told to go back
where we come from.
Years later the thanks we got was detention and
deportation.
Why oh why!!
Was this always part of their plan?
Burnt their papers they have no leg to stand
They can't prove that they have the right to stay in

this land.
Discrimination, deportation,demoralization from
leader down to baby in pram.

Jesus Jesus

Jesus Jesus how I love thee.
How I trust you more and more.
Jesus Jesus blessed saviour, you are all that I
adore.
Jesus Jesus my redeemer, mighty God of God, for
evermore.
Jesus Jesus most powerful presence, here from
dusk till dawn.
Jesus Jesus strong and steadfast hallelujah praise
your name.
Jesus Jesus merciful and forgiving our hope for life
eternity.

The Morning Lullaby.

Within the confine of my hospital room,
My mind all wrap up in chain,
I wish I could calm my brain.
Sweet music eco in my ears from the early morning
bird songs
The seagulls venture so far from their coastal home
to sing celestial tune
Oh, the heavens have opened!
The calm of the sea, the tranquil horizon,
Here, a vision of beauty seen from my bedroom.
With peaceful attention I listen so gracefully
meditating on how lucky I am.
I embrace the sight in my minds eye as the fishman
bring in their catch
The seagulls all greeted them breakfast is here they
sings to each other
Happy to partake in sharing the abundance that the
Lord has served.
A joyous feeling of wonder overtook me, I am now
fully ready to welcome the day.
My spirit is lifted, my mind is at ease, my hospital
bed is no longer a restraint.
My morning lullaby was tonic for my brain, pills for
my pains and holy water to break my train.

The Wooden Box

The wooden box seems a mile high
My two year old statue needs help to peep in.
Standing on a perching **stool** I come to notice the
stillness through the glass
Top of the wooden structure.
Resting precariously on its temporary legs
On that bright summer day
Proud and surreal in the front yard
A wooden box, a great man lying still,
Robbed of thought Robbed of movement
A box for a home
The end of time for the great man
A wooden box, is this the end? Or is it the
beginning?
The wooden box that almost reaches the sky.
Sleeping beautiful sleep.

What say us?

How far does our pound goes in the twenties
We work hard but can't buy plenty
Try with our might to put something aside
We seem to always lose the fight
For oh! My dear chap! the penny is tight
We talk of better for this decades
We strive to have that stock for our rainy day
How wrong we were as our pound loss it value
We now face the storm with empty arms
This is what is deemed double trouble Mr Prime
minister, what say you?
Let's balance the scale, we say to you, we don't
fancy the euro, the dollar we don't do
The pound in our purse, only that will do, get the
number right and ease our plight so we can all put a
few pounds aside.

Tek weh no fi yuh

Flush them out dem light finger without a doubt
imagine mi surprise when mi open the case
mi frock gone
without a trace you want to se the look upon mi
face
mi seh 'man the people dem is such a disgrace'.
Mi a fi come out a di place.
Mi seh gal before me loose me draws mi head fa
the gate.
No looking back
mi so angry mi feel to put up a plaque,
Stay away from wa use to be mi favourite hang out
fe satan a dance in on out with handful a cloth
And wa ever no nail down a fi him
Mi seh you want to se him a kick pupa licking down
the lane
One ting fi sure
mi nah come ya again.

My Twilight Years

I dream of living to a ripe old age
A mongrel, a Cheshire cat or even a cockatoo
Sharing salmon or two
Making a right halabaloo without little care
Of the uproar it triggers when we do
To John, Jill or sister Catherine who live just a door
or too
Oh! but now it's clear to me dreams are for dreamer
With eyes wide open it plain to see
The reality is knitting bunnies, mittens and drinking
Many cups of tea, with my mongrel on my knee.
Twilight years, is that what it call? What a laugh!!
Give me a couple glasses of whiskey and a knee
up, a night with my head over the toilet bowl ah
what a wonderful twilight year that would be not too
far fetch for me and auntie Maggie.

You are running the Hackney Half Marathon No way!!!!

Yes, I am, YAY!

Eight months ago
I woke up one morning with this light bulb moment
100 watts of energy beamed directly from my eyes
before I registered.

Oh my overactive brain cells.

Then the excitement begins
A phone call later I was on the list of people running
the marathon for Mind charity.
My fundraising page began
The dollars start rolling in from my connections
across the waters.
The pounds then follow.
No turning back now
This is looking like serious business
But I got this.

I recruited friends and family to help me with my
training.
This takes much planning as Covid19 prevents us
from mixing in groups.
I started by running but it proved to be too much for
me with my breathing difficulty
And the effect it had on my joints.

The fundraising was surprisingly good.
I have to rethink this:
I know I will have to walk this
Getting an asthma pump after choking in my sleep
after an emergency later landed me in the hospital.
Many tests later which are still ongoing.
Feet treatment, nausea and cataract operation.
Not forgetting postponement
The day finally arrived.

I was ready but so was set backs
All the roads were closed off on route to the starting
point because there was a marathon,
So no buses, so you've guessed it, I will have to
walk the two miles.
Well It was buzzing when I get there I was on cloud
nine
The atmosphere was electric.

Sonia, you did it!
You are ready
The excitement was hard to contain.
I soak it all up.
Time to get to the starting post
Now the job begins.
Started nice and easy, everyone cheering with
happy smiling faces.
Seeing friends and family earlier starter on their
way back
We all started at different times to stagger the
numbers.

All going great
One of my friends joined on her bicycle riding
following me.
Little did we know how crucial that would become.
It was like I was running for weeks, I was eating
fruits, sweets ,
Taking water and my pump
But my leg was giving way, I was dizzy, and couldn't
focus.
The bus shelter was where my friend help me to lay
down I remember seeing the six miles post Before,
so I know I was halfway there I know I have to carry
on
My friends raise the alarm
Contact family and friends who contact other.
Half way down the road it happened again
Lost my footing Go to the St John first aid
They give me tube of sugar solution, water and take
my pulse
Put the chair together so I could lie down. They get
me going again.
More friends joined us.
I was on my way again.
People were cheering me along and saying you can
do it.

They were taking up the barriers, opening up the
road saying to me go on the paving. It will be safer.
I was the only one still doing the marathon.
It was like the whole of Hackney, my family and
friends out to make sure I got to the finishing line.

Angel was left, right and center.
I made one more stop, just 3 more miles to go.
People bring seats out of the shop, buy me cake.
Family and friends get me coffee with caffeine,
Lucozade.

I use the little girl room and begin the journey to my
glory of achieving my goal.
The end of the marathon was exactly as it began,
the atmosphere, the excitement.
My heart was beating fast. I was praying as much
as we did along the way but much, much more.
Medal placed around my neck, I breathe easy,
smile and pose triumphantly.

THANK YOU LORD, WE DID IT !!!

Trust You?

I loved loved loved with eyes closed I lost big time!
I did not see when to shut the door

I paid the price with pain
I paid the price by becoming insane
I paid the price by being afraid of my home

Trust You?

Fear of my phone
Fear of being alone
Not knowing who is who
Fear of everything that was once me
Total loss of my identity

Building back trust,
I have begun
My eyes are wide open
My boundaries are set
My armour in place

Trust You?
Trust Me!!

The future is in my hands
I alone come on this land
Building trust is part of my plan
With me, My number one fan.

We got no wifi

WiFi?
What WiFi?
Talking about crawling the tortoise could get to
London and back twice before you could load a
picture
Charging phone don't let me start,
did you mention hours don't let me laugh

Weekend, yes the whole weekend to move 10
mins!!
Can this be the norm my heart bleed for the
suffering these poor
people going through
technology a non starter
The broadband provider is counting their dollar.
Me
I am just counting down the minutes when I can get
back to reality
and get my first true injection of WiFi overdose,
mind blowing tech,
more than I can digest.
Oh what the heck
I will eat some rocks have my fill of that great
staples
cod and chips
A healthy pint of beer, cockles, muscles, pickles eel
and a dip in the
sea.

Now that I am forced to go back in time, so far back
there was cousins
oil lamp
And outside toilet.
Technology of the future was just another number
eleven On Bill Gates
tens fingers

Crying silently.

Crying silently.
Mind body and soul ache
Do I forgive,
Do I forget,
Do I seek revenge,
Do I love,
Do I hate,
Crying silently.
Who caused the pain,
Me you I am going insane,
Don't need you
Messing with my brain,
Stop playing wicked games,
Crying silently.
Battered and bruised,
Bearing the scar,
Hurt betrayed,
Lied to, laughed at,
Wearing the fool's hat,
Crying silently.
Do I answer my silent cry,
Do I curl up and die,
Do I shout no more will I,
Do I put a stop to this cruelty
No more no more,
Crying silently.

He is a flirt.

He is a flirt.
Wearing my leather skirt
John pull me don't in the dirt
To my surprise he does nothing
But I guess he's up to something
Then John catches Sam, as I look around,
I heard, why are you!! pulling me down into the dirt?

Myself

My dear friend,
I empathise with you,
Last year this time I was in a dark, dark place
myself.

Could not see my way clear, so I begin focus and
ways
To practice some self help,
Caring for myself.
After speaking to someone
My whole life was lifted to the most magnificent
height.
I began to look at myself!!
Me-no longer a cocoon but a beautiful butterfly.

Young-stay young of mind and make sure I find and
implement new ways to keep it going.
Stop-take a good look at what I was doing wrong.
Erase-begin to get rid of self-doubt and stop
beating up myself.
Learn-learn new things and ways of dealing with
problems.
Find my voice.
You see me now, I haven't got all the answers,
But MYSELF has become my true energy.
My dark, dark place has an energy bulb.

Jamaica

Lover dream, pleasure seeker dream, dreamer
dream,
Jamaica the land of paradise,
The winding road,
The deep blue sea, from land can see,
Such magnificent view upon the horizon
Where the majestic skyline kisses the calming sea.

The ocean wave caresses the glistening silver sand
along the beach
Sparkle mile and mile around the land.
The island, perfect symmetry,
Taste as exotic as the eyes dear to adore
Of food that make such a wonderful chemistry.

Street walking venders of the Native,
with produce suspended high on head
On top a cotter support,
A vision of beauty no camera could capture for sure
do we, could we all afford to take a step with in
paradise that's where we want to be.

Jamaica is the land for me.
Market beaming rainbow bright.
Stall aroma put your nostril on full alert
Sun so hot make people ditch skirt and shirt.

Lord it made me so happy just buying some ackee.
Every day I had to shout

Jamaica I am glad
You are the land of my birth, mi so proud.

About the author

I am a mother of three, grandmother of nine and great grandma to one. I am truly blessed - thank God. Grown and raised in St. Catherine Jamaica in Spanish Town, I was looked after by my great aunt - Aunt Dine and her husband Mr. Alex in a working class family. Aunt Dine was a higgler woman selling oranges in the market whilst Mr. Alex worked in the cane fields. I came to England July 1973 at the age of 17 and had my first child. I left home in September and the rest is history...My poetry writing started at St Barts Hospital London when I had one of my many series of mental breakdowns. The staff in the mental health department encouraged me to write and they would type up my poems and I would frame it - my first poem was Imagine. I would write whenever I relapsed using poetry to express my feelings. It spiraled from there into something I would do in good health, I write about my feelings, family and experiences. I hope you get as much pleasure out of reading my book as I have had writing it.

Sonia B.

My first book, Within A Mental Mind gives an account of the happy and sad moments of my life and how I saw myself then.

My second book - Second Time Around is about my more happier and fulfilled life experiences. An insight into my world now and how I view it.

My third book, A rabbit in the sky of me, oh my, is a children's book about a group of unlikely companions who have adventures in the sky. It highlights diversity and overcoming adversity. It is a warm hearted tale with soft and unique illustrations.

This, my fourth book Poetry in Lockdown is my reflections on the happenings over our restricted movements.

Printed in Great Britain
by Amazon

34479868R00032